HOW TO KEEP AN AMAZING HEDGEHOG PET

**Featuring 'The African Pygmy Hedgehog'
Everything You Need to Know,
Including, Hedgehog Facts, Food, Cages,
Habitat and More.**

by Hathai Ross

Copyrights and Trademarks

Disclaimer and Legal Notice

Acknowledgements

I cannot thank my family enough for once again fully
supporting me in my journey in writing this book. I could
not have done it without them. I would like to dedicate this
book to my Mum and Dad who live in Thailand who I have
not seen for 3 years!

Contents

Introduction

The Hedgehog – As how we don't know it

Perhaps many young people nowadays would be familiar with the word "hedgehog" from Sega's internationally famous flagship character, a blue speedster who loves collecting golden rings. This leaves most of them surprised when they find out how hedgehogs are in real life.

However, for a majority of animal lovers, hedgehogs are known to make great pets. Normally weighing only around 2 pounds at the very most and taking up about as much space as a guinea pig, hedgehogs do not make any type of disturbing noise such as a bark or squawk. They are favorites of people who generally do not have time to care much for pets, but would like to own one as a valued companion – they do not have the same propensity for chewing through things as their rodent counterparts (such as hamsters), and they do not generate as much mess as other conventional pets. They are safe to be near children as they do not shed dander or any similar substance, and they are not aggressive despite the way they look.

No wonder several millions of people own hedgehogs, and they even have several pet clubs dedicated to them!
This book will help you learn every essential thing about hedgehogs, starting from high-level overviews to details that might not be so obvious. It will help you discover how to care for hedgehog as pets, know what hedgehogs eat, and many other hedgehog facts.

How to Keep an Amazing Hedgehog Pet

Chapter 1 - What are Hedgehogs?

Hedgehogs are small, insect-eating (insectivorous) creatures that live in many grassy landscapes such as savannas and croplands, generally avoiding forested areas. They are scattered around different countries around the world, and are native to England and other parts of Europe, Africa and Asia. Despite not being endemic to the American continent, a certain species, the *Atelerix albiventris* or the African Pygmy Hedgehog has been kept as a pet by millions of American households.

Many people still mistake the hedgehog for the porcupine, an animal that is different and (despite its similarities in features) is completely unrelated. Porcupines, known for their unique form of protection, possess sharp and dangerous quills that are absent in hedgehogs. The latter animal instead possesses smooth quills. Touching them would be just like touching a hairbrush or a similar implement – it feels bristly, but not prickly.

Normally, an African Pygmy hedgehog would average at around 1/2 to 1/4 pounds, ranging anywhere from 5 to 8 inches long, the same length as that of an average guinea pig. There are some hedgehogs that have been known to grow over 1 3/4 to 2 pounds even without exhibiting any issues on obesity. There are also those that are so little that they weigh only around 6 to 7 ounces. They possess an oval-shaped body, and females of the species are known to be typically larger than the males. They have short legs and tail, a long nose and small eyes. They also possess prominent ears and whiskers, both easily noticeable and denoting that the animal has been gifted with good senses.

The African Pygmy Hedgehog is also known as the "four-toed hedgehog", going by this name to refer to the number of toes that can be found on each of the animal's rear feet. While most other hedgehog types have five-toed rear feet, the African Pygmy variant only has either a stub of small, bony lumps or nothing at all in place of its hallux or big toe. There are some instances, however, that find an African Pygmy hedgehog sporting five complete toes on each hind foot.

The species' color can vary widely in coloration, but those that can be found in the wild bear spines that are colored brown or gray, with either a white or cream-colored tip. The fur itself is usually colored a speckled gray, with a brown hue just around the muzzle. It possesses a white face, legs, belly, and other underparts. The spines are always found on the upper part of the body, and range from 0.20 to 0.67 inches in length, with the longest being found on the upper surface of the hedgehog's head. The spines themselves can constitute as much as 35% of the hedgehog's total weight! They are composed of solid shafts, another marked difference from the porcupine quill which is hollowed out like a feather. These spines are laid down flat when the hedgehog is calm and can be petted smoothly when stroked from the front to the back.

The head of a hedgehog has an interesting feature, a furrow which naturally parts the spines on this part. This allows the hedgehog to raise the spines on its head when it is

How to Keep an Amazing Hedgehog Pet

mildly irritated or nervous, without them crisscrossing when the skin is pulled up over the pet's eyes. The furrow on the animal's forehead provides a space for the raised spines.

A hedgehog's snout contains anywhere from 36 to 44 teeth. These animals have a first pair of incisors that are slightly larger than the rest of their dental features, but not much so that they are dramatically different like rodents' incisors. Also, unlike rodents, these incisors do not exhibit continuous growth. This removes the innate tendency to gnaw on things to wean the front teeth. Like in humans, their baby teeth are shed to be replaced by permanently rooted adult teeth.

Generally hidden under their quills are short stubby tails that are seen on both sexes. For those inexperienced with caring for the animal, this tail may be mistaken for a penis in males as they are seen to curve towards the hedgehog's head when it is placed on its back. The penis of the male hedgehog is seen on the middle part of its abdomen. It is usually hidden within a penile sheath.

Unlike ferrets, hedgehogs do not have a scent gland within them, and so they do not possess any peculiar body odor. Even their urine does not contain a markedly high amount of ammonia, which can be found in the urine of rabbits and guinea pigs.

The hedgehog has a generally extensive range, as mentioned previously, and a stable wild population, leading the IUCN (International Union for Conservation of

Nature) to rate it with a status of "Least Concern". Currently, the taxonomic community has not yet agreed on a universally accepted subspecies of the *A. albiventris*.

How to Keep an Amazing Hedgehog Pet

Chapter 2 - Is a Hedgie for you?

Most people new to having hedgehogs as pets might not know one of the more elaborate reasons behind the animal's popularity in exotic pet trade. Many people breed hedgehogs extensively for their color and their temperament, much like breeders do for prized dogs and horses. However, despite the many advantages towards owning this exotic pet enumerated at the start of this book, it is still highly recommended that a potential owner check on the following possible downsides of owning a hedgehog.

First of all, a hedgehog may not be thoroughly advisable as a household pet if it is to be kept in a place easily accessible by children. A hedgie has strong defensive instincts, and may use its quills to poke your young ones. They are usually shy and quite nervous, not the type to come when being called, or to actually display any form of affection in the manner of dogs and cats, let alone do tricks.

As hedgehogs are naturally sleep creatures, they are best suited for owners who are asleep during the day. One may find hedgies doing little aside from balling up all day.
Hedgehogs also have the potential to bite (as any creature with teeth does), although this is actually done more often as a means of communication. Hence, it is important for the owner to thoroughly understand the behavior of his pet to prevent any risk of injuries.

We have previously discussed that hedgies are solitary creatures, so they are not for owners who wish to keep multiple animals in the same cage or shelter. At best, such an owner can opt to keep female hedgehogs, as they are the only ones who may safely co-inhabit. If a hedgehog ever becomes sick or injured, visits to the veterinarian may also be quite costly. They are also not the type of pets you could expect to survive on their own when left alone over the weekend.

Because of their natural adaptation to the warmer African climate, hedgehogs are best suited for temperatures ranging from 70 to 80 degrees Fahrenheit. Additional heat sources are to be provided to make sure your hedgie is at his most comfortable even during the cold winter months.

And finally, you need to check if your state, town, or county has passed a ban on owning exotic animals. As hedgies are considered "exotic," they may fall under this restriction.

Hedgehog Behaviour in the Wild

First of all, it is important to see how a hedgehog acts in the wild in order to understand how he is expected to act when brought home as a pet. It is to be understood that all animal behavior that may be exhibited comes from their natural instincts bred in the wild. Even though they have never actually been to the wild with their kind, genetic memory creates inborn instincts that will simulate wildlife behavior even in captivity.

African Pygmy hedgehogs are usually solitary, and are most active during the night. Although we can only see them at home traveling along the surface of the ground (their cage), in the wild they are capable of climbing and swimming whenever necessary, hinting at their active lifestyle. Their feet and toes are especially made for both running and walking. It is very energetic for its small size, and it has the capacity to go through several miles of its habitat in a single night! During their nocturnal activity, they forage for food consisting of insects, snails, grubs, some types of plant matter, and spiders. As well, their body has a very high tolerance for certain types of toxins – hedgehogs have been reported to consume some types of venomous snakes and scorpions.

As with other animals, some sounds may also be heard from hedgehogs, particularly snorts, hisses, and a quiet type of twittering. Whenever they are attacked, a hedgehog can scream loudly, and the males of the species can also produce certain bird-like calls specifically for courtship purposes.

In their daily activities, hedgehogs do not rely much on their sense of sight. This is a poor part of their senses, partly due to their burrowing nature. Compared to other animals like dogs and cats, they possess limited binocular vision and may have a hard time perceiving depth. This leads them to take falls from dangerous heights because they are unable to tell how far from the ground they are. However, they compensate for this weakness with other sharpened senses.

For example, a hedgehog has an excellent hearing faculty. Their defensive sense can be triggered by any unfamiliar or loud noises coming from their environment. They also have a great sense of smell that can be very useful when searching for food or in detecting danger. They even possess an uncanny ability to detect surrounding motion, even when they are unable to see (such as when rolled into a ball). In this state, any movement perceived by the hedgehog is interpreted as danger. Even while they are sleeping (or trying to sleep), hedgehogs are able to detect and react to any unknown movement around them.

A peculiar trait (at least among household pets) of the hedgehog in the wild is that they undergo estivation during the summer season. "Estivation" is the state in which animals become dormant during summer (equivalent to winter's hibernation), evidenced by a lower metabolic rate and inactivity. Usually, this state is initiated by a drastic increase in temperature characteristic of the season, forming arid conditions in the environment. However, it has been noted that hedgehog estivation is not really due to the heat itself but due to the associated lack of available food. Hedgehog estivation does not normally last for more than six weeks.

When threatened by predators, a hedgehog's standard defense (like its porcupine lookalike) is to tense up all its back muscles, causing the spines on its back to stand erect. Then, it rolls into a ball that protects its limbs and its head, with the aid of its orbicularis muscle that contracts like a drawstring. If the threat still persists, it twitches its muscles in an effort to jab the offender with its spines. It also makes grunting and snuffling noises to try and intimidate the harasser. Unlike the porcupine, a hedgehog does not leave its quills in the skin of its attacker. In fact, it is rare even for adult hedgehogs to lose quills – if this ever happens, it is often taken to be a sign of poor health.

One particularly queer hedgehog habit is what is known as "self-anointing". When the animal is introduced to a particularly strong odor, or some scent in his environment that he is not familiar with, he would react by licking or nibbling on the source of the scent, working up a lather of frothy saliva in its mouth. Then, the hedgehog makes a particularly queer effort of spreading this froth to all areas covered by its spine. Until now, no conclusive evidence has been presented regarding the reason for this behavior.

There has been some laboratory research published indicating hedgehogs may be doing this to spread poison or any of the unknown substance on their quills, making them more dangerous to predators. In the experiments, hedgehogs given a poisonous marine toad to self-anoint with automatically went for the poison gland, demonstrating their outstanding resistance to neurotoxins.

Also, poor diet can cause the hedgehog to exhibit tooth decay and symptoms of gum disease.

Overall, a hedgehog's lifespan in the wild is a bit shorter at only around 2 or 3 years. Most often, a hedgehog will die because of predation and not because of old age. Studies have found no statistical difference between hedgehogs of opposite genders.

Is a Hedgie for you?

A female hedgehog can produce litters composed of anywhere from 1 to 9 hoglets (baby hedgehogs). The time between their conception and the time of birth (gestation) is around 33-35 days. Hedgehogs can typically breed just after six months from birth.

In Captivity

Like all animals that are retrieved from their natural habitat and placed in the care of us humans, hedgehogs will display the same characteristics as they do in the wild. Their active lifestyle might be the aspect most impacted by any form of captivity, which is why they are usually placed in pens larger that those usually allocated for other species of the same size. They are also to be provided with exercise wheels to augment this. Some owners have estimated that their pets travel upwards of five miles in a single night, with speed exceeding almost 10 miles per hour in bursts. Though their feet are best developed to help in such sprints, owners are advised to trim the nails on the front feet more frequently so that they do not grow long enough to damage the foot pads.

A hedgehog's senses may also be able to adapt to the noise of a busy household, but it may take some time. Hence, the animal's defensive sense may be triggered by different sounds at first. Hedgehogs are naturally defensive and will thus need proper handling and care to remove or weaken the automatic fear that might pervade. Like other animals, hedgehogs can sense the variation in their owner's emotions, and can relax more quickly when their handlers are confident.

How to Keep an Amazing Hedgehog Pet

Their defensive measures stay the same, and may coil up from a provocation from its owner or any other person. A hedgehog's lifespan in captivity has been measured to last anywhere from 4 to 6 years. Also, when kept in a place that has more regulated temperatures, hedgehogs do not estivate even in the summer months. When kept properly, they have been shown to be hardy animals. However, some hedgehogs have been shown to be vulnerable to tumors as they mature.

Hedgehog Talking

We have previously mentioned that hedgehogs are not very vocal, unlike the other household mainstays like dogs and cats. However, like most other animals, they also emit certain sounds that can serve as clues to their current mood. It is to be emphasized that the information contained in this section is not an absolute truth for all members of the species. As responsible pet owners, it is up to us to actually know about the current status of our pets, drawing from our experiences and other interactions with them.

Hedgehogs are individual creatures that might differ in the ways they express their emotions, but listed here are the most common interpretations that can serve as a guide.
Sounds such as the squeaking of new baby hedgehogs, like the sounds produced by newborns of other animals, may not mean anything specific. However, an owner may tend to ignore small sounds such as clicking, popping, or any similar things. These last two may actually be a sign of discontent, signaling that your pet has gone into defense

mode. It would be a good thing to look at different ways to handle your pet better.

This annoyance may also be conveyed by a series of huffing, puffing, and sneezing sounds. It may be a good idea to approach differently, or to keep your distance from your pet in the meantime. In contrast, a hedgehog grunting may mean that he is contented, or is enjoying your company. This same affection goes with a purring or whistling sound, like cats do.

When sick, they may also emit such sounds as sneezing, snuffling, and wheezing. If this is the case, it is best to check them for any illnesses. However, some hedgehogs may also use these sounds as a means to get the attention of their owners.

We have mentioned previously that hedgehogs are solitary creatures and do not like sharing cages even with their own kind. If you happened to ignore this fact, the most prevalent sound you will probably hear is squealing – the surest sign that a brutal fight is going to occur.

The last and most dreadful sound a hedgehog may emit is a scream. It is the sign of either extreme pain or fear, caused by fighting, any injury, or any outside factors. Hedgehogs are also knows to emit this sound even while asleep, for reasons yet undiscovered – possibly, a type of nightmare is being experienced.

Is a Hedgie for you?

You are a Perfect Hedgehog Owner If...

There are people looking for the perfect pet, but here we are also going to look at some of the characteristics of the perfect owner for this remarkable species.

Of course, first on our list of must-be's would be a **knowledgeable** person – the more an owner knows about hedgehogs, the more he can easily understand his pets and attend to their needs. Being **patient** is also another key aspect, as an owner needs to be persistent in order for him to gain the trust of his pets – and hedgie trust does not come in an instant. Being **gentle** is also another aspect of this patience. To be sure, gaining your pet's trust is a rewarding experience.

A good hedgehog owner, like those who own other types of animals for pets, should also be very **observant**. Your pet will depend on you for each and every one of its needs. You will need to understand the subtle communications your hedgie is trying to convey.

As well, a good owner should have a degree of being **financially responsible**. Owning a hedgehog wouldn't be cheap, starting from its acquisition to the veterinary care it would require at least once in its entire lifetime. Food and other supplies should also be provided properly.

A hedgehog owner should also be **accepting**. A hedgehog would not be the type of pet to offer tricks or to follow commands. It has very little to offer in terms of those aspects. However, a hedgehog derives its charm not only from its quirky habits, but from the affection it may share to its owners.

Finally, a hedgehog owner needs to be **thick-skinned**! As hedgehogs employ their peculiar brand of self-defense, a good owner should not be afraid of being pricked once in a while. A hedgehog is not for the person who is afraid of being bitten or spiked.

Some experts have found that a hedgehog is best raised as a family pet, wherein adults, more than children, are involved in its care. It is important to have an adult eye in observing the hedgie, from its eating and activity levels to its temperature and health. In contrast, youngsters may have their attention taken away from the pet and into extracurricular activities.

As well, some hedgehogs may do poorly as classroom pets as they are not supposed to be left alone over the weekends. Taking the hedgie home with various students during school year breaks (such as in the summer, or in semestral breaks) would not be advisable as well, as these changes can increase the risk of problems that may ultimately result in death.

However, a hedgehog may be a great instrument used to stimulate learning. They may also serve as an exceptional form of animal therapy.

Chapter 3 - The Hedgehog Connection

Being a pet owner is a very exciting prospect. It is akin to bringing in a new member of the family. You welcome it and allow it to acclimatize in its new environment, making sure that it is warm and comfortable, while having easy access to its food and water. You allow it to rest after bringing it into its new home. It is actually most advisable to put in the exercise wheel only after the second or third day. Make sure that they are able to establish a good feeding and eliminating pattern before adding stimulation. It is also important to keep other animals away for the meanwhile, to reduce your hedgehog's stress.

Hedgie Handling

There are some people who suffer a nasty nibble the very first time that they handle their new pets. This is but natural behavior, as hedgehogs will mostly want to take a sample bite if your hand smells just like some food item it knows! The very first thing that an owner should learn before handling a hedgie is to properly wash his hands. This is preferably done with a neutral-smelling soap. This helps protect you from unwanted bites.

Most hedgehog enthusiasts would recommend handling your pets for at least around half an hour a day. The most acceptable time of the day when handling your pet may vary, so it is up to you to understand your hedgehog's behavior.

Another tip when picking up your hedgehog – do it steadily and confidently. Do not be afraid, and do not hesitate, but don't be too fast as well. You will not want your pet to feel threatened and roll into a ball. Since a hedgehog has an excellent sense of movement, it will detect any irregularities in your manner of picking it up. The more confident you are in handling your hedgie, the more comfortable it will be with you.

A good handling technique will be to pick your pet up evenly with both hands. At first, it will roll into a ball. As time passes, they will then learn to relax when picked up by their owners. If you are being pricked consistently, you might want to use gloves when picking your pet up.

As you pick up your hedgie, it may let its curiosity get the better of it and start wondering about its situation. This will lead a curled hedgehog to unfurl. Once they do this, they have the very likely tendency to start exploring – in fact, some may do it right away and actually walk off your hands! Once they do this, make sure to put the other hand in place to give it a new platform to walk on. There may also be the shy ones who will start by sniffing and will duck at any hint of a noise.

When petting your hedgie, make sure t do it from front to back to avoid getting in the way of its spines. Some may not like it at first, but will respond appropriately when you earn their trust. There are even those who will root for petting, by snuggling close to you.

Litter Training

A litter pan is considered by many to be an essential part of a hedgie's cage. It helps save time and effort cleaning droppings provided the hedgehog uses it accordingly.

Ideally, a litter pan should have a low front that the hedgie can climb in easily. It should also have room enough for the pet to climb in completely and turn around. Make sure to place it as far away as possible from the food and water supplies. The best way is to usually place the pan wherever the hedgehog always uses the bathroom. Inside the litter pan itself, it is recommended that a different substrate than the one used in the bedding should be placed.

Although technically, no hedgehog could be totally relied on in the use of their litter pans, a little coaching may do the trick. The best way is to actually place some droppings on the pan as a cue that they should use it when defecating. There are also owners who catch their hedgies at an appropriate time just as they are getting ready to defecate and put them on top of their potty place. This may be effective, but it is up to the owner to determine what will work best for him.

Bathing and Trimming Nails

Many hedgehogs actually enjoy their bath time, especially when in warm water. Some enjoy themselves too much and they tend to relieve themselves while still in the water, which an owner should watch out for. There are owners who prefer to bathe their pets in sinks or bathtubs, since it will be easier to change water there. Remember that even though hedgehogs can be good swimmers, it is never advisable to leave hedgehogs alone in the water without supervision.

Unlike other animals, hedgehogs do not groom themselves. Thus, it is up to you to bathe it regularly. Remember, though, that too much bathing can also cause symptoms of dry skin to appear on your pet.

When bathing a hedgie, you will need some mild soap such as tear-free baby shampoo (or even a homemade oatmeal soak), warm water, a soft toothbrush for brushing the quills, and warm water. A small piece of carpet under the one- to three-inch water will help your hedgehog from slipping too much. It also helps by providing friction to clean the feet and toes. After bathing, you may use a dryer-warmed towel to keep your hedgie warm. It is not advisable to use the dryer directly on your pet. To prevent chilling, make sure that your pet is thoroughly dry after bathing.

For the nails, a hedgehog's nails are basically similar to those of humans. Some less active hedgehogs may regularly need to have their nails trimmed, at around every two weeks. There are also those more active ones who wear out the nails on their own at play. Long nails can curl under and be the cause of deformity and damage to the hedgies' feet. They can inhibit walking was well as increase the risk of being infected.

Baby nail clippers are found by some to be the best means to trim the nails, and some may see that a bath would leave the nails softer and easier to cut. This also usually leaves the hedgie more relaxed. You may cut the nails easily by asking someone to hold the feet while you do the trimming, or by letting the hedgehog grip tight on a screen that is tilted at an angle, so you can pick up a foot and trim it on your own. Cutting too far into the nail bed can cause temporary (but relatively harmless) bleeding, which can easily be stopped by any blood-stopping product. Cornstarch or flour is also a good alternative.

Playing Hedgies

Though not typical, some hedgies might still end up chewing through electrical wires. Thus, it is best to keep these out of sight when letting your hedgie explore the surroundings while at play. Even litter box training may be nullified when the pet gets the urge to explore outside of the cage.

Places with surrounding walls of smooth sides are best since there is little chance the pet can get away out of hand. Plastic kiddie pools are ideal, unless you have placed items close to the walls. Hedgehogs have been known to give themselves a boost by climbing through accessories used for play.

You may also bring your hedgie out on a warm sunny day, but make sure to keep the perimeter guarded so that your hedgie does not scuttle off unwarranted.

Many enthusiasts have found out that hedgies love to play their own version of the game hide and seek. They are capable of hiding for hours and days on end. If you wish to find a hedgehog playing this game, your best bet would be to go down on your hands and knees and look for dark and warm places your hedgie may be taking as a refuge. Such places are refrigerators and stoves.

As much as possible, do not place your hedgehog in a room where there are couches or similar furniture. Another person may come in and unwittingly sit on a hedgehog that happened to be lounging there.

Hedgehogs may also sneak behind cabinets, even drains and ducts. This warrants extreme vigilance to make sure they do not venture into one. If a hedgehog seems to be winning a game of hide and seek (I.e., you are not able to find it within a day), you may place food and water inside a paper bag – once the hedgehog searches for food, you will hear the bag rustling.

Remember that hedgehogs are nocturnal creatures – many an owner has had to search for hedgies in the dead of night with a flashlight. If you do not want to go through such an extremity, it is best not to let hedgie play the game in the first place. Or, you may cheat by having nowhere to let the hedgie into hiding.

How Hedgies Know

You might be wondering how, given a hedgie's poor eyesight, it is able to distinguish among people to know its owner. Like most animals, hedgehogs have very strong sense of smell. It can memorize your scent "fingerprint", and thus know if you are around. But aside from merely knowing each other from an owner-pet relationship, it Is very important that bonding takes place. It requires love, persistence, effort, and an intellectual understanding of hedgehog behavior.

One of the best ways to let your hedgehog familiarize itself with your scent is to wear a single shirt all day that will be draped over your pet's cage for the night. You may also stop using artificial scent-enhancing products while around your hedgehog such as perfumes and soaps with strong scents.

With their excellent healing faculty, they may also recognize the way you speak. Talk to your pet and let it be familiar with the way you speak. It is best to do this while performing such acts as petting, kissing, bathing or snuggling. Hedgies may also respond favorably to radio and music. The constant stream of sounds on a radio will help your hedgehog remain unobstructed by new sounds it may hear. If a hedgehog is used to the silence of being alone, they may consider the simple opening and closing of a door to be noise, making them nervous each time it happens.

For those who are not into such actions as snuggling, one of the easier ways of bonding would simply be holding your hedgie on your lap while watching television, or something similar. If your hedgie is still shy, you may not be able to pet it just yet. Just simply let it relax and come out on its own. There are many scientists who suggest letting your hedgehog stay close to your chest until he can feel your body warmth and hear your heartbeat. You may let it sleep on you, as this is an excellent way to bond with your pet. It is also a good opportunity to pet an otherwise grouchy hedgehog.

If you have more time on your hands, it might also be a good idea to simply set your hedgie loose within a safe area, allowing it to take its time and get to know you on its own terms. You may place your (washed) hand around a foot away from the hedgehog, allowing it to come up to you. It might actually climb up on you and explore – let him do it. It is best to learn how your hedgehog reacts to subtle changes in the area, including temperature, noise level, and even color.

As well, like in cats and dogs, one of the most effective bonding weapons would be a handful of treats!

Chapter 4 - The Signs of Good Hedgie Health

A responsible owner should also be able to attend to the health of their pets. Fortunately, diagnosing the overall health of a hedgehog can be relatively easy. An owner would best start with the eyes - these should be wide open, clear, bold, round and bright. A hedgehog's eyes should not be sunken, watery, or dull. As well, they should not have any discharge, regardless of the color or viscosity.

The hedgehog's nose should also be checked. Like most other mammals, a hedgie's nose is supposed to be moist and clean. It should not bear any traces of being bubbly, running, or dry.

The ears should also be looked into - they should be clean and without any form of drainage, crustiness, or flaking on the lobes or the outer part. The skin as well should not exhibit any abrasions, or any lumps and bumps. The last two are of special attention, since it has been established that one of the leading causes of hedgehog death in captivity is cancer. Any lumps should therefore be taken immediately for diagnosis. Excessive dryness should also be watched out for, as well as any form of bare patches or signs of mites and other parasitic insects.

The fur is another matter to be thoroughly checked. A hedgehog's fur is supposed to be completely filled throughout the sides, without any signs of being matted, especially for the underbelly. Some hedgehogs might have a streamlined appearance, but their skin should always be tight and filled out entirely below the ribs. For those

How to Keep an Amazing Hedgehog Pet

plumper hedgies, they should not be so fat that they are unable to easily roll into a ball for self-defense.

Breathing should also be regular, as in humans, without any sign of stress. It may be easy for first-time owners to confuse a hedgehog's normal huffing behavior with the rattling sound of a respiratory disease. It is also ideal for an owner to track the food and water intake of his pet, in order to properly assess any improper loss or gain of weight. The bowel movements of a hedgie should be similar in color to the food they had previously eaten. Keep a watch for green-tinged droppings or excessive bowel movement (diarrhea), as these are sure signs of either illness or stress.

As for the hedgehog's movements, these should be free without any signs of wobbling or limping. A hedgehog should not be dragging its feet when it moves from one place to another. It should be noted that a hedgehog's normal gait is bound to produce a "pitter-patter" sound on the surface of the cage.

Maintenance Work

Like all household pets, hedgehogs would need some form of maintenance so that they are always at their peak. Generally speaking, different hedgies may require different levels of care depending on their individual habits. Most often, working with hedgehogs would involve spending time on keeping their cages and their bodies clean.

Basically, the most rudimentary things an owner can provide to keep his pet happy are fresh food and ample water, coupled with regular (weekly, or so) cage cleaning. Hedgehogs, despite being very active, are not the type to go for walks. They also seldom need to be bathed, unless they accumulate dirt on their feet and quills. Overall, a hedgehog whose cage is properly maintained and who is fed a good diet will not smell as much as a dog, cat, or similar conventional pet. Hedgehogs are also neat when it comes to their elimination habits, and will regularly use a litter pan if provided. They regularly do their own body cleaning by licking, scratching, and shaking themselves.

Despite all these, an owner should not take the easy care of hedgehogs for granted. As in other pets, certain issues may appear that could worsen when neglected, or when the signs are taken for granted. One should always keep a close watch and take care of concerns in a timely manner.

Hedgehog Diet

African Pygmy hedgehogs are known to be insectivores in the wild but they also may be resourceful enough to feed on carrion (dead bodies of other animals, in a similar manner to vultures) when nothing else is available. They may also eat birds' eggs, lizards, snakes, or similar small animals that it happens to catch.

Before, cat food was the only type of food available to hedgies that have been domesticated. However, advances have been made since then on the different components of hedgehog nutrition, allowing for commercial hedgehog food to take cat food's place. However, not all of these products are equal in their quality and nutritional value, much like other commercial food available for other pets. Even now, cat food is still being used as a substitute. However, those who do so should be careful about the nutritional quality of the hedgie's fare.

Hedgehog and the World

It is but natural for pet owners to keep their hedgehogs in a home that houses other animal species. Though a hedgehog is solitary, it can be compatible with other animals depending on the personality of each. Also, it is important for the cage of each pet to be kept safe and secure from the larger ones (such as cats and dogs) until the owner is sure how they will interact.

As a rule, all interactions between pets should be completely supervised until one is sure that they are safe with each other. For example, a hedgie may be in complete danger when a hunter cat or dog is in the house. The hedgehog should never be used as a toy or plaything for other larger pets. Those among other species that may come across as overly curious may cause the hedgie to be scared or intimidated, which we would not want. In worse scenarios, even smaller animals like rats may impose damage by biting and chewing on a hedgie's quills.

In contrast, other pets may feel instantly intimidated by a huffing ball of prickles, especially when they get on the wrong end of their quill jabs. This should be enough to have most dogs and cats remain at a safe distance. There are also instances when a hedgehog may form a close bond with your other pets, to the extent that they are actually playing and sleeping together.

Another wise thing to remember is that bacteria can travel almost instantaneously among pets. What is normal for one pet may not be so common to another, and diseases may occur. A trend may be seen (though there are no official studies as of yet) among families that also own a bird or a type of reptile - these animals may transmit a higher rate of bacterial infections to hedgehogs, including Giardia, Coccidia, and Clostridium.

Another thing that all hedgehog owners (and virtually any pet owner) should be aware of is the possibility of zoonotic diseases. These are illnesses that can be transmitted from animals to humans. Any animal has the potential to act as a carrier of diseases. Hedgehogs are not known to act in this manner, although they possess a different set of flora that are completely alien to humans in a natural environment. As such, young children, elderly people, and anyone who has a compromised immune system may be at a greater risk for possible medical concerns. The best way to combat this risk is to make sure that all who handle the hedgie properly wash their hands afterwards. This especially applies to younger children who are more prone to putting their fingers into their mouths.

Chapter 5 - Hedgie Diet

As previously discussed, hedgehogs are natural insectivores. In the wild, a hedgehog has the capacity to eat anywhere from 1/3 to a whole hundred percent of their body weight in insects in a single night. They can eat the whole insect, regardless of it having a hard exoskeleton, although they do show a preference for soft-bodied ones such as centipedes and millipedes.

Hedgies are also shown to be able to eat some seeds, vegetation, and soft fruit. However, their bodies are not really designed for such a diet. Hedgehogs lack what is known as a cecum, the lower end of the colon in other animals. Herbivores have a fairly developed cecum that contains bacteria, aiding in the enzymatic breakdown of cellulose and other plant matter. In contrast, carnivores only have a small part of this cecum, called the vermiform appendix. The tendency to eat plant matter is probably caused by a shortage of the hedgie's natural diet in the wild. When provided with enough of their preferred food, however, a hedgie will not be a threat to any plat matter when freed in one's garden.

The Hedgehog Mix

Most of today's knowledge about hedgehog diet and preferences come from research activities conducted by Dr. Graffam-Carlsen hailing from the Bronx Zoo. Her research was presented at the 1998 Go Hog Wild convention that gathers hedgehog enthusiasts.

How to Keep an Amazing Hedgehog Pet

Her research verified that like humans and most other members of the animal kingdom, a hedgehog is in need of a blend of basic nutrients: proteins, carbohydrates, minerals, vitamins, fiber, and water. Their insect fare is eaten whole for this purpose as well. Most breeders have found that the protein content eaten by hedgies should be at least greater than 20% to produce a healthy specimen. For growing babies and their nursing moms, breeders usually feed them protein sources at around 28-35%.

In contrast, the fat content should only be at around 5-15% for the average pet. Nursing moms and their babies may benefit from a higher fat level, but maintenance food should carry less than theirs.

Generally, insectivores eat around 15% worth of fiber. However, most foods typically do not contain this amount of fiber. Just like us, it will be beneficial for hedgies to have an added dose of fiber in their diet. When feeding a hedgehog with food of higher moisture content, more fiber is needed. This applies especially for those who feed their pets canned cat food. In contrast, those who are fed a dry diet typically are not in need of such high fiber levels.

The Big Blank

Despite all these knowledge, there are still aspects of the hedgehog diet that are unknown to us. In fact, diet is still one of the most debated topics in the field of raising hedgehogs. All that we have are studies, and some of them may be inconclusive. And, despite the ever growing number of hedgehog enthusiasts around the world, no one is still perfectly sure what the hedgehog really wants or needs. Different individuals of the hedgehog species may need different types of nutrition, to suit their body types, metabolic levels, activities, and various stressors. It is also a limiting factor that on the global scale of pet ownership, hedgehogs are not yet on the needed popularity scale (at least in comparison to more mainstream pets such as cats, dogs, hamsters, etc.) in order for the needed definitive scientific studies to be taken regarding their diet. A thorough study would necessarily include a large population of hedgies, running over a long period of time under controlled laboratory conditions and followed by a set of complicated statistical analyses. Many would find that there have been relatively few advances made in the field of hedgehog diet research since Dr. Graffam presented hers.

As a general rule, breeders and enthusiasts recommend feeding your hedgie a variety of foods. This is probably the safest and most effective way in order to meet a hedgehog's unique nutritional requirements. This variety is mostly kept by using the hedgehog's staple food in conjunction with nutritional treats as supplement. This is also useful so that your pet will not be attached to just one food. It would be a serious problem for any pet if he refuses to eat anything but his favorite – and the mentioned food runs out or you are unable to provide it.

Hedgie Standards

Another thing all hedgehog owners should know is that the standard of food quality for animals is different from that of the one used for humans. Food can generally range in qualification from those that are highly processed and mostly artificial to those that are certified organic. While we would certainly consider human-grade and thoroughly organic foods to be better, keep in mind that this is not what most hedgehogs would eat in the wild. We have previously discussed that hedgehogs also eat carrion or dead animals, including their fur, skin, and bones. Together with their regular diet of whole insects, they are likely to ingest a fair amount of debris such as soil, making for an entirely different classification. Although of course, it would not be advisable to feed your hedgehog items from road kills, it is to be kept in mind that valuable nutrients may be gained from food matter that is considered unconventional to us humans

When thinking of which food to buy for your pet, it is very important to look at the list of ingredients. Always make sure that your chosen food should contain the following two characteristics:

Appropriate Protein Sources.

These should be high quality, and should always be in the top 2 ingredients found in the list. Items such as chicken, chicken meal, and lamb are usually the best protein sources for insectivorous animals like the hedgehog, since these items are most easily digested. While pork and beef are cheaper protein sources, they are not as easily absorbed. Also, those food items that contain different protein sources are more likely to provide more benefits, as they can provide a wider variety of amino acids. These amino acids serve as the building blocks of all plant and animal cells.

Appropriate Protein and Fat Ratio.

Like in other pets, hedgies may require different levels of fat and protein levels at different stages of their growth and development. As mentioned previously, those hedgehogs that are at a maintenance level would need less protein than growing hoglets or their mothers nursing them. Because hedgehogs are active creatures, more fat may actually benefit them, as it provides more calories for them. But like always, excess fat content in food can cause obesity and similar health problems. It helps to know that many pet foods are available in their regular and "lite" forms, the lite form being used mostly when the pet is at maintenance levels.

It is important to check on the size and hardness of the food that is being fed to our pet hedgehogs. Keep in mind that hedgies have smaller mouths when compared to other pets such as cats and dogs, and they are not capable of picking up their food to nibble on them as rodents can. Larger sized kibble should be shred or crushed to smaller bits. It is possible for a hedgehog to be malnourished even when fed good food, simply because it is too large or hard for them.

Some crunch in the food may be beneficial in that it helps to clean the hedgehog's teeth, similar to what insect exoskeleton can do when they are in the wild. In fact, a diet composed of entirely soft food can lead to tooth decay, and some gum diseases. In contrast, very hard food can wear down of totally damage a hedgie's teeth. Some hedgies are no longer able to eat when they have missing or damaged teeth.

The No-Nos in Food

There are also some things that a hedgehog diet should not contain.

Peanuts, Sunflower Seeds, and other seeds and nuts.

These food items are best left for rodents or birds, as hedgehogs are not equipped with a mouth , tongue, or front paw that is specialized enough to help them crack and eat the meat of the seeds. These foods are serious hazards that can cause choking. At the very least, they may have the peanuts stuck in the roof of their mouths. It is to be noted that some brands contain nuts and seeds in their food and treats.

Dry Fruits and Vegetables, including Raisins.

These food items sound good in theory, but actually may do more harm than good for your pet. Raisins, in particular, tend to stick to the tiny teeth of your pet, causing tooth decay. Dried vegetables, on the other hand, are hard to chew and to digest. It is best to read the ingredients label of food carefully, as some brands sold also contain dried fruits and vegetables.

Meat By-Products, and other Generically Listed Components.

These include designations such as "meat and bone meal", "poultry by-products", "animal fats", or "animal proteins". These items should always be specified to ensure your hedgehog gets the best out of the food you feed him.

The Controversy on Corn

Corn, an extremely popular food fare for humans, has recently become a controversial component for dog, cat, and even hedgehog food. There are those who have come to the conclusion that corn actually has little to no nutritional value (at least for our pets), and are only acting as fillers for food products. Therefore, they assert that corn should not be given a place in our pet's carnivorous or insectivorous diets.

This might fall as counter-intuitive, however, as corn is still one of the staple dietary components of a lot of meat producing animals in farms, such as cattle, poultry, hogs, goats, and sheep. It is still considered as a protein source, and is also blended into other animal feeds. Needless to say, it is also a staple part of the human diet.

There are those who take on the stand that it all comes down to the quality of the corn itself, how it is processed, and which part of the corn is used that will ultimately determine the nutritional value of the actual product. This goes the same for the assessment of many hedgehog owners, who have elected to keep corn as a part of the hedgie diet, but only in moderation. It is advised that this should not be the primary ingredient or protein source in your pet's food. Many owners still maintain that excluding corn products from their pet's diet could not be nutritionally justifiable.

Dog Food, Cat Food, Hedgehog Food

No manufacturer of any product would label their item as "junk". This goes out as well to those companies who venture into the production of pet food – not because a certain food item is labeled for a certain animal does it mean that it is ideal (or even good) for that certain species. Certainly, items marketed as "hedgehog food" would be a gamble for reasons previously discussed. This is the reason many people still opt to feed their hedgehogs quality dog or cat food as a means of sustenance.

Very few hedgehogs in captivity were ever raised on a diet of cat food alone. One of the reasons for this is practical – not many can afford to feed their hedgehogs top-quality cat food all throughout its entire lifespan. Another reason is that hedgehogs are insectivores, and are not meant to subsist entirely on a carnivorous diet.

As for dog food, perhaps one of the biggest disadvantages would be the size of the kibble. This applies even to the "bite-sized" varieties. However, high-quality crushed dog food may form a suitable part of a hedgehog's diet. One of the main differences between dog and cat food would be that cat food contains Taurine, a nutrient that is essential for cats but not for man's best friend. It is still largely unknown whether this nutrient has any effect to the overall health of hedgehogs.

Generally speaking, some of the most palatable treats for hedgies come from canned dog or cat food. When thinned and slightly warmed, they can be delectable for your pets. They are also good for hedgies with missing teeth or other health concerns. Like mentioned before, though, soft foods do not provide the necessary tooth abrasion that harder foods can provide. Also, moist foods cannot be left for more than 4 hours out in the hedgie's cage so that it will not be a medium for bacterial growth.

The Most Important

Like in humans and in other mammals, there is a single most important ingredient that should be present in all of a hedgehog's meals. This is **water**. Fresh water should be available in the hedgehog's cage at all times.

If you are using a water bottle to give your pet a drink, it is ideal to daily check the water flow in them. Sometimes, the bottle may become plugged or the ball itself may be stuck in an odd position that can impede water flow. Also, always make sure to change the hedgie's water on a regular basis, as stale water can grow harmful organisms that may affect your pet's health. There are also hedgehogs who will drink very little or refuse to drink at all if they happen to not like the taste of the water. If this happens, they are very susceptible to fatal kidney complications. Hedgehogs should not drink less than two ounces of water in a single day, and it might be essential to use filtered or bottled water if your hedgehog refuses to drink what is provided him.

Some hedgehogs may also spill the water in bowls you may be providing them – it is important to clean these as you may have a problem with mildew or molds in your pet's cage.

Monitoring Intake

In pets, one of the most common signs of a health problem would be a sudden change in the animal's eating or drinking habits. Proper eating should lead a pet hedgehog to reach its adult size after only half a year. It is best to keep a tab on your pet's weight on a regular basis to make sure that they do not lose or gain any excessive amount of weight.

Once a hedgehog reaches adulthood, it might be advisable to lessen the amount of food that he is fed in order to prevent the onset of obesity. Health problems relating to diet appears to be one of the most prevalent concerns for many hedgies and their owners. In fact, obesity has been found to be one of the most often-encountered problems in hedgehog raising – many hedgehogs die in a state of obesity. Another diet-related issue would be Fatty Liver Disease, one which is caused in much the same scenarios as in human instances.

Remember that some food items we may consider feeding our pet hedgehogs (kitten food, ferret food, wax worms among others) may be significantly high in fat and calorie content. Exercise, aside from proper diet and limited calorie intake, is also essential. It's a good thing hedgies can get active on their own! A good way of providing a good mixture of exercise and feeding to your hedgehog is by scattering their favorite food across the cage floor. This way, they are encouraged to "hunt" for their treats, allowing them to burn calories in the process.

Something New?

There are times when we would like to introduce something new when feeding our pets. Remember that we have to be very careful, as some food items may produce allergies or other unwanted reactions, such as green tinged fecal discharge. Introducing new food for hedgehogs should be similar to the way we introduce new food for human babies. Only one food should be introduced at a single time, over a period of 2 to 3 days in a week. This way, any unwanted effect can easily be diagnosed as to which of the food items caused it.

Remember that fresh food should be fed in the evening, when the hedgehog starts his activities. If there are any portions that were left uneaten, remove them first thing in the morning.

Like humans and most other animals, hedgies will always have their own taste preferences. Some hedgehogs will like to eat a different type of food periodically, while some will stick to eating nothing but their staple diet. Still, there are those who will not eat unless presented with their favorite food.

Just like human toddlers, a hedgehog may take liking for a specific food item if it has been offered to him several times. Younger hedgehogs may have a better tendency to be more accepting of new food items that their older counterparts. Like people, a younger hedgehog would not be set yet in its ways. Always make a good record of your pet's food preferences, and its effects on your hedgehog (health, weight, appearance, even on the hedgie's fecal droppings). There are some food items that may not be healthy when presented daily (but those that our hedgehog may really like). These foods may come in handy when your pet refuses to eat anything else.

Treating Them with Love

Giving treats to pets is of course a given, but it is best to hold on to those kibbles at least until your hedgehog has completely settled into his new home and started eating on a regular basis. At around 8 to 10 weeks from birth, a hedgehog would be ready for your offerings. Since they are natural insect-eaters, freeze-dried insects may be given at an earlier age.

Like their diet, hedgies may have the tendency to be picky with their treats. Some of them will love it, while there are those who will stick to their dry staple food. It is important to introduce only one new type of treat at a time, just like in his main diet. The same logic applies – if your hedgehog suffers from any stomach upset, at least you will know which food item is to blame. And like snacks, make sure not to stuff your pet too much with treats that he becomes too full to take his regular diet.

A treat becomes a treat because it is something special, something that cannot be found in the hedgehog's normal diet. Never overfeed your pet with treats, so that he is not psychologically conditioned to expect them as a standard part of his daily diet.

Normally, the foremost reason treats are given to pets is as a means of providing variety to their daily fare. For more mainstream pets like dogs and cats, these food items may also be used as a means of enticing them towards performing a certain behavior. It is also used as a means to foster a bond with your pet. This said, it is also important to consider treats that provide nutrition, as these are better than those that only provide taste.

Here are some suggestions for perfect hedgehog treats.

Insects.

As hedgehogs eat these primarily in the wild, they will surely eat them in captivity. In fact, insects serve as a mandatory part of a balanced hedgehog diet. Most hedgehog owners feed their pets such insects as mealworms, wax worms, crickets and silk worms. They may be live, canned, or freeze-dried.

However, it is to be observed that a diet based purely on insects would not be complete, so they are mostly restricted as treats. If you are going to purchase insects from anywhere, make sure that they are recently fed or "gut loaded". Insects that are not properly fed are nothing more that empty husks, usually imbalanced in phosphorus and calcium. It is always best to feed your hedgie store-bought or farm-raised insects instead of their wild counterparts, to avoid the risk of parasitic infection or other issues.

Meat.

Hedgehogs are never supposed to be fed raw meat, because of the risk of salmonella poisoning. Only feed them meat as long as these are broiled, baked, grilled, boiled, or microwaved. They should not be seasoned, and should be cooked with oil or butter.

Cook the meat until tender, and cut into small pieces that can easily be ingested by your pet. Some favorites as observed by hedgehog enthusiasts include salmon, chicken, and turkey. Beef and pork are also fine, but should always be fed in moderation as they are less easily digested. They also contain lower levels of calcium as well as higher levels of phosphorus than other meat alternatives.

Again, meat is not supposed to be a major part of the hedgehog's diet. Meat without supplements would run your hedgehog through the risk of calcium and mineral deficiency, as well as tooth problems for lack of proper tooth abrasion.

Egg, Rice, and Tofu.

Most hedgehog raisers have found that their pets take a liking for scrambled or hard-boiled eggs. If you will do the same, the best way to accomplish this is through the microwave without adding any oil or other seasonings. Make sure that the eggs have cooled sufficiently when you give them to your pet.

Fruits and Vegetables.

This would be a common idea for most beginner hedgehog raisers. However, like mentioned earlier, hedgehogs are not thoroughly equipped with the digestive faculty to break down the cellulose in plant matter. If you ever decide to feed this combination to your hedgie, it is best to stick with the fruits as they are typically easier to digest.

If you have nothing else but vegetables, make sure to dice them into small pieces that are either microwaved, boiled, or steamed so that they are soft enough. Certain hard vegetables including carrots and sweet potatoes should *always* be cooked as they pose choking hazards when served inappropriately. Corn and peas, popular fares for humans, contain excessive phosphorus that may result in decreased calcium absorption. Hence, they should only be fed in small amounts.

Some popular fruits and vegetables include apples, banana, strawberries, watermelon, mango, cucumber, asparagus, bell pepper, and turnips.

Baby Foods.

Though we can never know the exact taste preferences of our hedgehogs, aside from gleaning the clues of their dietary habits, they might actually enjoy the taste of baby foods. These food items have the advantage of being relatively inexpensive and easy to store. Several flavors, such as meat in gravy, fruits and vegetables, meat sticks, and chicken and applesauce have become popular with hedgehog raisers.

Some "higher stage" baby food (i.e., for older babies) may contain added sugar, salt, and other spices or ingredients that may be harmful to your pet. These food items should be avoided.

Cheese, Yogurt, and other Dairy Products.

Some hedgehogs may be lactose intolerant, especially the adults. However, yogurt and cottage cheese may be good alternatives that are found to be fairly easy to digest. They provide a much-needed calcium supplement for your pet, and yogurt also provides beneficial bacteria that can aid the digestive process.

Cat food and Ferret Treats.

These non-human food items may also be used, as they are relatively cheap as long as they do not comprise the entire diet of your hedgie.
Just as there are these treats that have been found to be beneficial to hedgehogs, there are also those that should be

45

avoided in all instances. These must-not's of hedgie treats are enumerated here.

Sweets.

Sweet foods typically contain a large amount of refined or processed sugars that can be deterrent to the overall health of your hedgie. As well, it is important to avoid giving your pet chocolate, no matter how tempting it is for humans. Chocolate has been found to be toxic to hedgehog and other types of animals.

Frieds.

Fried foods contain grease that is likely to upset the stomach of your pet. The additional calories are also not good for those hedgies who are above their normal weight bracket.

Hard and Sticky Foods. Raisins and other sticky food may stick to the teeth or roof of the mouth, causing discomfort at the very least and tooth decay in worse cases. Hard foods such as raw carrots, almonds, and such are choking hazards.

Stringy Foods.

These foods are mostly coming from the vegetable and meat group, and may be hard to chew or digest by your pet hedgie.
Raw Foods.

This includes raw eggs and raw meat. The risk of salmonella infection is serious, and can be aggravated by not cooking the food prior to feeding your hedgehog.
Spicy Foods.

Food items containing a large amount of onions or garlic, or other strong spices may be bad for your hedgehog's stomach.

Salty Foods.

Aside from the possibility of upsetting your hedgehog's stomach, salty food can also cause electrolyte imbalance that it detrimental to your hedgie's health.

Got Milk?

Hedgehogs may also suffer from lactose intolerance, just like humans and many other animals. In fact, Dr. Graffam's research has said that many adult mammals are not really designed to digest milk very well. Therefore, we should refrain from giving our adult pets too much of it.

One can see the signs of intolerance from stomach and intestinal problems, indicated by frequent bowel movement (diarrhea) and foul-smelling stool. Once this happens, it is best to stop giving any milk-based substances. Yogurt is a great substitute and is easier for hedgies to digest than milk. It is also beneficial as it provides a good source of calcium.

There are a lot of hedgehog care guides that suggest low-fat cottage cheese and different types of cheeses as alternatives. This is fine, as long as the animal does not exhibit any ill effects towards the fare. Monitored feedings should start with small amounts.

Don't Fill Up

There are those owners who buy food with different types of fillers, typically if they do not take the time to read the ingredients list. Studies have linked these fillers and other preservatives to different types of illnesses, ranging from cancer to ear infections, respiratory diseases and joint problems.

If ever you will purposefully add fillers to your hedgehog's diet, study it very, very carefully. Some of these have undergone different processing procedures and may therefore contain low-level chemicals, some of which are not even supposed to be food-grade!

Fiber is a good and natural filler that you can use – in fact, some hedgehog food manufacturers have elected to use fiber from soy hulls and other healthy products to increase the nutrition value of the product. These fibers are naturally provided for in nature. Other fiber sources include whole grains, those that are also advocated for a healthy diet in us humans. Always remember that processing plays a very vital role in the production of healthy food products – different grades of nutritional levels may be produced from the same product, simply because of differences in processing.

Hedgehog Supplements?

Yes! You can feed your hedgehogs specific food supplements to ensure they are always at peak health. There are also certain scenarios when food supplements are extremely helpful. For example, fiber is a great addition to any diet. It can be achieved by adding hedgehog bite-sized pieces of grape nuts cereal (not the nuts themselves!), Benefiber, or baby oatmeal.

Stinky Droppings?

Anything that goes in must eventually come out. The same goes for whatever your hedgehog eats. All hedgehog droppings smell in one way or another, but it is up to the owner to determine "how bad".

The most effective way to reduce the smell of your pet's fecal discharge is to make sure you keep track of everything your hedgie eats. Different foods will have different effects on the hedgehog's fecal quality, and closely monitoring what they eat allows you to adjust accordingly. Many hedgehog foods will offer free samples that you can try out.

Refusal to Eat

For any pet owner, perhaps one of the worst parts is when your pet suddenly refuses to eat. Going on a hunger strike can be an effect of various symptoms such as sickness, environmental changes, change in diet, or even change in temperature.

In these occurrences, it is important for the owner to get their pet up and eating once again. This is, of course, after we check that there are no outward signs that our pet is caught by an illness. Any obvious signs should immediately be looked into by a licensed veterinarian. It is also best to check the temperature of the cage, as this may be the source of the refusal to eat.

Start by tempting your hedgie with the food it likes the most. You may also soak these treats in low-sodium chicken broth, to present a more tempting mix. Sometimes, canned cat food will also do the trick. You may also scour the Internet for a lot of recipes that hedgehog enthusiasts have compiled in order to jumpstart your hedgehog's appetite.

If this fails, you may need to take your pet to a veterinarian for check-up. This is especially true if he stops eating for more than a few days, or if he also stops drinking.

How To Feed

You may also be wondering about the most effective way to give food to your pet. Feeding hedgehogs actually comes in different ways, with different tools that can be used. Some of the most common ways of feeding are discussed here.

Hand Feeding.

Many would argue that this is the most "personal" way of feeding and can best be used to foster a closer connection between you and your bristly pet. However, hand feeding is not recommended for beginners, as the hedgehog may take the next natural action and bite the feeding hand. This is actually a natural response by handfed animals who are looking for more food (case in point: the bears at Yellowstone). On the contrary, your hedgehog will not be as tempted to bite anyone's hand if it starts to associate food with any inanimate object.

Feeding Bowls.

Crocks or plates are useful in order to separate the food from the floor of the cage, and also enable the hedgie to find it easier. Small containers are ideal for this task.

Feeding Tongs.

Many animal caretakers use feeding tongs in order to avoid the risk of being bitten. This is especially true with reptilian species. It can be said to be a good compromise between owner safety and having a personal hand in the feeding of your pet. One of its advantages is that the hedgehog learns to associate the food with the tongs, something inanimate, instead of your hands. It also prevents the smell of food from clinging to your hands, reducing the hedgie's temptation of biting it while you pet him afterwards.

Dropper or Syringe.

This is especially useful as a means of administering such food items as yogurt or baby food. This is also used for sick hedgehogs, as they may have to be dropper fed for them to ingest any food of medication. It has been observed that if a hedgehog learns to accept treats through syringes, they will most likely not put up any fight should they need any syringe-administered medications or supplements later on.

Unlimited Feeding vs. Monitored Feeding

Among hedgehog enthusiasts, there are as many different opinions on whether unlimited free feeding would be better than daily monitored feeding sessions. There are those owners who hold the belief that hedgehogs are supposed to have food in front of them at all times, for them to eat whenever they feel like it. These people believe that it is not in the habit of hedgies to overeat on their own. It is worthwhile to note that certain hedgehogs (babies, nursing mothers, or those that are slimmer than the normal type) should really not be restricted as to the amount of food that they take in – but at the same time, their intake should be closely monitored.

There are also enthusiasts who have found that feeding your hedgehog once a day would suffice. It is a good way of controlling obesity and all other health problems associated with it. This is similar to many diet plans that are in place for us humans. Monitored feeding should also allow an owner to monitor when the hedgehog suddenly stops eating.

Free feeding would entail letting food sit in the hedgehog's cage continuously for a number of days. This requires little in the way of planning the necessary amount. However, monitored feeding should be planned carefully, so as to not lose its advantage of offering fresh food each time the hedgehog eats.

Technically, food is determined to be enough if it is completely gone or almost gone after around a full day from the time it was left in the hedgehog's cage. It is vital to observe the next meal onwards, to make sure that the food you left is not too little – your pet should not eat like it was starving the next meal. Depending on the hedgehog "enough" food may mean anywhere from 1 tablespoon to ¼ cup. The varying factors include the level of metabolism, its current growth stage, the activity level your hedgehog enjoys, and the quality of the food itself.

There are also those owners who prefer to feed their hedgehogs smaller portions of food, but at an increased frequency in a day. Normally, hedgies will adapt to any feeding time within the day or night, but it is still important to be consistent with the time you feed your pet.

Food Storage

Like in keeping food for humans, it is vital to keep the food for your hedgehog fresh. This will help in protecting the integrity of the food, its nutritional value, and its palatability. It would be helpful to purchase a food storage container from your dollar store or any variety store. You may opt for a container with a screw-top lid to help protect the food.

You may want to store a portion of the food in a container close to you hedgehog's cage. This is meant for any time you wish to feed your hedgie some treats. You may place the rest of the food in the refrigerator.

Another good idea is to start creating a food log so that you can track how frequently you have to purchase food. Certain food manufacturers also have a toll-free number that you can keep handy for restocking.

When purchasing large amounts of food, you may want to put the bulk of it in the freezer. Make sure to keep it in a vacuum sealed. Whenever thawing the food, move it first to the refrigerator rather than directly bringing it out to room temperature. Moving it to the refrigerator first will prevent the formation of condensed moisture which might cause the food to spoil.

Chapter 6 - The Bug Eater's Life

We have repeatedly talked about how important insects are to a hedgehog's diet. This section will explore this further, allowing us to understand deeper the role insects play in the totality of the hedgehog's eating habits.

It should be noted that hedgehogs in the wild may have different nutritional needs than those that are in captivity. This does not, however, mean that their dietary preferences may change greatly. The difference in requirements mainly comes from the large difference in the activity levels of wild and captive hedgies. Mostly, wild hedgehogs are able to adjust their dietary intake depending on the nutritional levels they need. In contrast, those who are captive can only rely on what we give them. And as e have iterated before, feeding your hedgehogs a straight insect diet would not be a good idea as it is usually unable to meet all of their dietary needs.

There are insects specifically raised by farms as feeders, and this is mostly recommended instead of those that are simply caught from the wild. Remember that feeding your hedgehog insects is tantamount to feeding them with whatever the insects have eaten before. This includes (in the case of those insects from the wild) parasite and other pollutants. Poisonous substances may also be found. Even if you do not use herbicides, pesticides, or similar deadly chemicals around your home, others around you may do so. These toxins may ultimately build up in your hedgehog's systems with the passage of time. In case you have previously fed your hedgehog any wild insects, it is

How to Keep an Amazing Hedgehog Pet

best to subject him to a de-worming process every set interval, same thing with what you do with your cats and dogs.

Another thing to be avoided is purchasing insects that have been raised to act as baits. These insects are usually raised on manure, whose impurities may be passed along to your hedgehog.

There are different ways you can feed insects to your hedgehog. These include those that are outlined below.

Live.

Though it may seem unwieldy, live insects actually provide a good level of environmental stimulation and enrichment for your pet. There are certain hedgehogs that are enthusiastic when it comes to hunting, and there are those that are downright lazy and would not make an effort to catch their food.

You may place your hedgie in a bathtub or a laundry sink, as these are great places to feed insects in. A hedgehog will eventually learn that he can catch insects when placed in such a place. For the owner, uneaten insects can also be easily caught.

It is best to remove any uneaten live insects after around 15 minutes. Remember that live insects will have to be contained and fed properly before they are fed to your hedgie. Insects that are not properly sustained will eventually not have the same nutritional content.

Freeze Dried.

Those insects that have been freeze-dried are also available from several suppliers. These are usually sold by weight, and are usually the cheapest. They have the advantage of having a long shelf life and of not smelling as bad as their canned cricket counterparts.

Canned.

In compensation for their strong odor, these insects are usually the juiciest. Though they may smell, they can actually be appetizing to your pet. One thing to remember is that canned insects have to stay in the fridge once opened. Compared to the freeze-dried ones, they usually have a shorter shelf life. Yet, these are still more convenient than any live bugs.

Keep in mind that one of the best measures of how good a food item is for your pet is nutrition, which should strike a balance with palatability. Generally, when an insect has high moisture content, there is a lower percentage of protein and fat. Below are some of the most common insect fare for our bristly friends, and their approximate nutritional value. Take note that some of these are not recommended food, but they are discussed as they are still being used by other owners. It will be up to your discretion to choose the best treats for your pet.

Crickets.

These can be purchased either live from pet stores or from insect suppliers in a canned or freeze-dried form. When opting for live crickets, they should be "gut loaded". This means that they should be filled with food that will ultimately be beneficial to the hedgehog. Crickets that have been gut loaded have a higher vitamin, mineral, calcium, and overall nutrition content than those that have not been properly fed.

Live crickets can also be killed or stunned before being fed to your hedgehog. This technique will suit the lazier among your pets. They can be stunned by placing them in the freezer for a short amount of time, or if you intend to kill them, they can be left there overnight.

When feeding freeze-dried crickets to your hedgehog, remember that they are quite brittle and should be stored inside plastic containers.

Live crickets should be kept in an aquarium or similar enclosure for keeping before they are used as treats. This should have a screen or mesh lid. You may also use cardboard egg crates inside their container so that they have somewhere to hide, preventing them from trampling each other. While in captivity, they should still be fed with a high-calcium diet and water in the form of carrots, a moist sponge, sweet potatoes, or even a specialized cricket gel.

Night Crawlers and Earthworms.

Though many people contest that they provide good nutrition for hedgehogs, feeding these items may result in negative effects for your pet. Many owners complain that these food items give their hedgies liquid, foul-smelling fecal discharge, and many also dislike the process of cutting them up into bite-sized proportions for your hedgie to eat. Another danger is that earthworms may carry threadworm or lungworm which can be transmitted to your pet. These are fatal and should be avoided at all costs.

Mealworms.

These types of worms sport a three-stage life cycle, much like a butterfly. These are larva, pupa, and adult beetle. The mealworms that are bought are in their larval stage (hence the wormy look), although all stages are edible for your hedgehog.

Raising a mealworm colony at home is fairly easy, and the Internet abounds with valuable resources that can help even complete beginners. All that is needed is some time and some extra space. They only need normal to warm room temperature and simple requirements when it comes to food. Feeder mealworms are best kept in the refrigerator, and maintained with high-calcium insect food as their bedding. They are refrigerated in order to prevent their transformation into beetles, as their larval stage would be easier to control.

Silk Worms.

These words are harder to find and are more expensive, but a hedgehog owner may find in them some benefits that make them worth the effort. Silkworms are generally described as undemanding and easy to care for, having a low mortality rate. They can last over a week without being fed. They can be grown easily to up to three inches or more simply by feeding them with mulberry leaves. There are also specialized silkworm feeds available in the market.

Silkworms are found to have a higher calcium and lower fat level than other types of insects. They also have a soft outer body, making them easier to digest. They are not the type who attempt to escape, and many hedgehog owner have found that even picky pets can like them as treats.

Slugs and Snails.

Snails caught in the wild may carry lung or thread worm, which as mentioned above cam be transmitted to your pet and cause deadly complications. Pet stores' reptile sections tend to offer safer, farm-raised, canned shelled snails.

Super Worms.

Sometimes called zoophobias, superworms share much of the physical appearance of mealworms. However, they are more than twice the latter's size, and can be much more aggressive than them. In fact, these worms have been known to bite their hedgehog predators – both before they are eaten, and after they are trapped in the hedgehog's stomach cavity! Some owners have reported their hedgehogs vomiting blood right after eating superworms, although there are those who consider this as a mere urban myth.

If ever you decide to feed your pet superworms, it is best to kill them first so they cannot bite back. The simplest way of doing this is to store them in the freezer overnight.

Wax Worms.

These worms are actually the larval stage of wax moths. They can be harder to find and are more expensive than other types of insects. They are also high in fat content, so it is recommended that they be used sparingly as treats.

Roasted wax worms smell a lot like peanut butter, and could easily pique you hedgie's appetite. Like mealworms, it is best to keep them in the refrigerator and on top of a bedding of high-calcium insect food.

After all these, you might notice that true hedgehog enthusiasts care not only for their pet hedgie but also for its food. They do this to make sure that their pet gets only the best treats. If you have time and can spare the extra effort, you may also take care of your own hedgehog insect food.

Since insects are not conventional pets (and are not even considered as pets), taking care of them can come across as rather unconventional. For example, they are not fed out of any dish but rather have their food as their bedding. A lot of commercial bedding options are available, and homemade ones can also be concocted. Stores that supply them also usually carry the needed food to sustain them properly. Caring for your own feeder insects will ensure that you also give the best nutritional value you can derive from them to your hedgehog.

Chapter 7 - How Healthy is your Hedgie?

Now that we have discussed diet, which is one of the most vital factors in maintaining the health of the hedgehog, it is also important to discuss the other aspects of a hedgie's lifestyle that allows us to determine how healthy your hedgehog can be overall. You may notice that these aspects are very similar to those lifestyle aspects we look into to be healthy as humans. Therefore, it will not be difficult to apply them to our pets as well.

Exercise.

As hedgehogs are very active in their natural habitat, it is also important to provide them an active environment even in captivity. This will allow them to keep fit. Many captive hedgehogs will still log miles on their wheels in a single night, similar to what they would do in the wild.

Exercising has been known to produce great benefits in a majority of mammals, and these are documented in countless researches all around the world. Exercise can easily be stimulated even in captivity by having owners provide their pets with ample space in their cages, a large wheel, and some time out of the cage in order to play. Hedgies who get this treatment are usually healthier and happier than their peers.

Bedding.

Hedgehogs lie close to the ground, and are always in contact with their bedding. In fact, their nose would usually be only around an inch or so above their bedding at any given time. This means that the air they breathe can easily be contaminated by the bedding they lie on. Bacteria and other impurities on the floor can be easily inhaled by hedgehogs.

Beddings made of soft wood (such as cedar and pine) are known to contain aromatic hydrocarbons that can cause respiratory problems and other types of diseases. Dusty beddings can also do the same.

You may also see some specialized beddings in the market labeled as "safe if ingested", although this can only be true in smaller amounts – anything in excess can surely harm your pet.

Some hedgehogs have been known to consume a large amount of bedding, especially when you switch between different types. This can lead to impactions, as well as other complications. Then again, some may cause skin problems, irritations, or allergies that in the end may cause secondary infections.

Aside from the obvious impropriety of keeping a dirty hedgehog bed, it is also important to know that this can cause ammonia buildup. This increases the risk of bacterial infections drastically. Other components of an improperly cared for bedding include molds, mites, and other pathogenic substances. There is no perfect bedding as of yet, ad different hedgehog breeders will always have their own choices. We will discuss more of these in a later chapter.

How to Keep an Amazing Hedgehog Pet

Genetics.

It is always recommended that people purchase only from registered hedgehog breeders, instead of from conventional pet shops. These breeders have a responsibility of producing animals that are healthy through and through using proper breeding techniques.

Breeding is always a very hot, and sometimes even controversial topic in raising any animal. There are several methods and styles, all of which have their own proponents and critics. There is cross-breeding, line-breeding, and there are even in-breeding practices, all of which have their ups and downs. It is important for the breeder to carefully select the breeding stock. This will benefit not only them, but also their customers. It is important to always start with quality parent hedgehogs - although the rules of genetics dictate that they will not have a 100% chance to also produce quality offspring. Purchasing hedgies from a breeder that is knowledgeable in this area, and who is also concerned about his produce will be infinitely better than nothing.

Breeding.

You may want to use the hedgehog you currently own as a breeder, it is important to know the consequences of this decision as it relates to your pet's health. It has been found that breeding female hedgehogs can greatly increase the risk of death and health complications. They can occur at any point starting from the breeding and all throughout the nursing process. Breeding poses a great stress on the body of the female hedgehog, and as such can lower her immune system drastically (like it can do to humans). When this happens, infections may find the opportunity to attack.

Stress.

Yes, stress can affect animals in just the same way it affects humans. In hedgehogs, it can be caused by anything that they deem unpleasant, from an unwelcome environment to outright danger. Stress, like many people say, is an integral part of life, and there is no such thing as something that is truly stress-free. Like in humans, you can easily see a stressed hedgie through certain signs such as nervousness, grouchiness, a change in stools, or simply through their defensive stance with all quills bristling up.

They have an extremely good hearing faculty, so they may be stressed because of sounds that we can barely hear or those that would rarely bother us. They may also be stressed because of the way they are handled. This is the reason why some hedgies are not meant to be classroom animals or educational aids.

The sad fact is that a lot of owners tend to abuse their hedgehog pets without even realizing it. There are even some people who roll hedgehogs like bowling balls when they are in their defensive stance. And lastly, like in humans, stress can actually be fatal to your pets.

Quality of Living.

It is not a mere abstract concept - studies have shown that happiness can actually help a person or pet live a longer life. Hedgehogs also need attention from their owners, no matter how much they enjoy being solitary. They will also need some form of environmental enrichment, and thus they need some time out of their cages as well. Those hedgehogs that are left in smaller cages with very little attention or care will usually succumb to more health complications than their happier counterparts.

Accidents and Injuries.

Even in the safest conditions and with the utmost care, accidents can happen. There are times when our hedgies may take a fall, and the injury might not be apparent at first. However, such accidents can cause internal damage that cannot be seen by the naked eye.

Like most pets, there can be times our hedgies may cause harm to themselves by ingesting substances around the, that can be toxic. They may also get trapped outside the cage, or may injure themselves with some appliance or item within their cages.

This the reason owners must exercise wise judgment in the selection of cages and other accessories that coexist with your pet. Supervising any play sessions will also help decrease the chance of accidents. And of course, be careful about your pet's interaction with other animals.

Diseases or other Illnesses.

Animals are all susceptible to infections caused by parasites, bacteria and a lot of other potential pathogenic substances. These occur throughout our lives. They may be passed on from one animal to another, from the owner to the pet, or even from the pet to the owner.

A strong immune system augmented by the proper diet and supplements, and good hygiene through frequent washing and disinfection have mostly been pinpointed as the best ways one can avoid potential diseases.
Each animal has his own collection of normal flora, bacteria that can be found inside and outside their body. These do not cause any diseases unless they exceed the tolerable limit. When new bacteria enter the body, disease is likely to occur.

There are a lot of illnesses or diseases that can be found in both humans and hedgehogs. These include those affecting the respiratory system, the urinary tract, digestive disorders, and even cancer.

Veterinary Care.

This is the hedgehog analogue to the annual visit to the doctor for check-ups. Aside from this, it is also important to get medical intervention as quickly as possible when we think our hedgehog has health problems. It is important to note that hedgehogs may actually hide any injuries, increasing the complication of trying to find it. In the wild, a small, sick animal can easily fall prey to opportunistic predators. This is the reason several animals have evolved the ability to outwardly hide any inner ailments.

How Healthy is your Hedgie?

An owner needs to be able to keenly observe his pet's actions, as a change in habits and mannerisms can usually be the first sign of ailments. If you are a new owner, it is most advisable to take your new pet to the veterinary for check up after 2-4 weeks. During this time, the pet needs to be comfortable with you, enough so that it can easily be handled and examined without causing it any undue stress. As the owner , you also have to build a rapport with your vet, in order to have someone you can call on in case of emergencies. This will greatly increase the chance of having a successful treatment.

Many owners have the habit of waiting until something goes really wrong before they take their hedgie to a veterinary. As a rule, it is a whole lot easier to treat any medical issue when it has just started, rather than wait until everything has come to a head.

Estivation and Hibernation

As mentioned at the beginning of this book, hedgehogs also undergo the process of dormancy during the changes in the season. Hedgehogs have the habit of building up fat reserves during the warmer months, allowing them to sustain a certain period of inactivity.

When in captivity, hedgehogs may also be able to hibernate whenever the season gets too cold. However, this is only a partial hibernation. Though this is a force of nature acting upon your hedgehog as a means of self preservation, it can actually be very dangerous as your hedgehog can simply die in this stage. Estivation during the summer for pet hedgehogs has been found to be comparatively rare, but may just be as dangerous. Therefore, hedgehogs who are living in captivity have to always be placed in a controlled environment in order for them to remain active whatever the season its.

The most common signs of estivation and hibernation include coolness to the touch, becoming lethargic to the point of being unable to unroll, or on the other hand not being able to roll up at all. If it does unroll, one may find it wobbly. Its appetite is also lessened, towards complete cessation of eating.

Hibernation can be triggered if the hedgehog's surrounding temperature goes down to 68 degrees Fahrenheit. Estivation, on the other hand, has been thought by some scientists to occur not because of a temperature change per se, but because of the lack of food associated with this change.

The best first aid for a hibernating or estivating hedgie is to reverse the temperature very slowly. Make sure to keep an eye on this change, as it may be too sudden for your hedgehog. You know you have succeeded when the hedgie starts to move around, and you are unable to keep it in just one place.

Once this is done, a visit to the veterinarian is due to make sure that the inactivity really was due to hibernation – it might be the first signs of a life-threatening ailment. Delay in the care for such illnesses may result in death. Take note that not all veterinarians treat hedgehogs, and it is highly advisable that you have one you can contact in case of such emergencies.

Upon ensuring that your hedgehog has warmed up sufficiently, make sure that precautions are made in order for this not to recur in the future. It is best to subject the room's temperature to control, monitoring fluctuations during both the day and night. Your cage may be placed beside a leaky window, resulting in it catching drafts from high winds. A digital thermometer may be a handy tool.

Quilling

Technically speaking, what we call "quills" on a hedgehog are not really "quills" – they are spines. They are nothing but hardened hairs that have a solid center and taper at both ends. They fall out just like regular hairs, and are replaced over time. In contrast, quills are shallow like a feather's shaft and have barbs on the bad end. They can be released at any time – which cannot be said for our hedgehogs and their friendlier spines. And yet, we will be continuing what we have started and call these bristly contraptions "quills"!

There are times when a hedgie will shed a large number of its spines, in a process appropriately known as "quilling". This is a natural process, much like the shedding of skin. Coats can be changed at any time of the year, although they are shown at specific times like in adolescence. Many have also observed that quilling occurs first after around 6 to 8 weeks of age, and then again when the hedgie reaches 4 months.

The first time quills are shed, one can usually find the loss of finer quills and the growth of newer ones. These newer ones tend to be thicker.

Quilling itself can be a clue as to the skin health of your hedgehog. For example, a quill that has shed naturally can be seen to have a bulb at the root, much like human hair. Those that shed due to an adverse skin condition or due to mites are found to have a flaky tip or a soft one on the edge of the spine.

Sometimes, hedgehogs might also need time to adjust to the quilling stage. Their pores are still relatively tight when still young, and would not always easily give way to wider quills. You might see a few quills that look like ingrown hair – marked by redness, swelling, or scabbing at its base. These spines might need to be pulled gently, and subsequently washed with a gentle cleaning solution such as mild soap to prevent infections.

The quilling process may be painful for your hedgie. It may be in the same way as teething for us humans. While there are those among them who do not show any discomfort at all, there are still those who tend to become very grouchy.
As owners, we should also have the responsibility to help relieve our pets of any discomfort caused by the quilling process. Instead of petting them, which is the usual comforting behavior, it is best to just let them crawl over you. We would not want to aggravate their pains by touching that already sensitive top layer. They may appear grouchy, but this grouchiness will also fade.

To make sure hedgehogs are at their most comfortable in this tender time, you may want to wash them with any oatmeal-based soap to make an oatmeal bath. There are owners who bathe their pets and then rinse them with something containing Vitamin E. Some have also found that a couple of drops of olive oil can help when placed directly on the skin, not the spines. It can help soften the skin, assisting in the quilling process. However, be mindful than an excess of olive oil can also cause problems.

An average hedgehog has around 5,000 spines on its body, 90% of which will be replaced in its entire lifespan. If you see that the quill loss is not due to the natural quilling process, it is best to consult your trusted veterinarian. Aside from the afore-mentioned mites, other factors such as diet, stress, and different types of hormonal imbalances can also be the cause of the quill loss.

Chapter 8 - Hedgehog Beddings

As previously mentioned, there has not yet been found a single best item that can play the role of a perfect hedgehog bedding. Each and every owner and most veterinarians may have their own varying opinions and recommendations.

This is compounded by the fact that the numerous available commercial hedgehog bedding materials all claim to be the best. As a rule, none of these manufacturers would label their products as something that is inferior or that can be toxic to any pet. However, with the proper knowledge, an owner will be able to assess the qualities of each material used for beddings, together with their benefits and the risks it can pose. Some of the major factors that can be considered include: appearance, accessibility, toxicity, and ease of cleaning. Let us not also forget the ever-important cost factor.

Keep in mind that whichever bedding type you choose, it plays an integral role in keeping your pet happy and healthy.

A lot of the paper, wood, and other types of processed materials used in bedding can accumulate dust. And yet handling them properly can reduce the amount of dust found in each individual bag. Fluffy beddings, on the other hand, can cling to your hedgie and make your floor quite messy. Also, fragrant types of bedding (mostly those with added chemicals) may cause respiratory issues. In contrast, a deeper layer used as a bedding can provide you the necessary room to scoop under your pet when picking him up, as well as provide your hedgie opportunity to burrow.

Keeping Health in Mind

Any responsible owner will think of the hedgehog's wellness and safety first when choosing any accessory to place in his cage. This applies to his beddings as well. Like us, hedgehogs may also suffer from allergic reactions to certain types of beddings. An irritation or rashes may be the first signs of these, although mites may also be the culprit.

Once they have been eliminated as theroot cause of the irritation, then it is high time to change your pet's beddings.

Speaking of mites, some hedgehogs may obtain them directly from the bedding itself. They may infiltrate the item at any of its various sources, from the warehouse itself to the pet shop where you obtained it. Although any maker can produce a mite-free product, they will be unable to control the surroundings their product goes through. It is important to check each bag or package of bedding you buy to ensure that it is not contaminated.

Also, as hedgehogs conduct themselves near the ground, their genital areas come into constant contact with the bedding. It is best to check to make sure no irritation occurs, especially since this may lead to urinary tract issues. Be careful about choosing dark-colored beddings as this may camouflage the color of your pet's droppings. This may not only make proper maintenance of the cage difficult, but it may also make it hard for you to observe fecal clues as to your hedgie's health.

As part of the fairly inquisitive nature of hedgehogs, they are prone to trying a taste of their new bedding. Typically, this would not be harmful. However, too much of this can cause an impaction of your hedgehog's bowels. Like many things, it will be quite hard to distinguish how much would be "too much". And yet, you should seriously consider removing the bedding if the simple curiosity leads to the hedgehog's substitution of treats for their new bedding! It will be best to introduce their new bedding gradually just to see how they will react.

Respiratory issues may also occur not only if the bedding contains dust, but also when it starts to break down.

Bedding No-nos

Given the health issues stated earlier, there are some types of beddings that should definitely be avoided.

Cedar Shavings.

It does not take much searching over different sources to find several warnings against the use of this type of material. Cedar shaving has been studied and has been shown to be harmful not only to hedgehogs, but also to reptiles and birds.

Cedar shaving contain the toxin Plicatic Acid, together with some other aromatic (or volatile, hence the danger they present) hydrocarbons and phenol compounds.

These same phenols have their uses - they give off a sweet scent and also repel insects such as fleas and moths. However, they also lead to issues in smaller animals - most notable, liver problems, respiratory illnesses, and some cancer types.

Cedar shavings can still be found in pet stores for use as filler in dogs' beds. Anything smaller than that could pose complications.

Sawdust, Hay, Straw, Soil, and other Organic Materials.

As mentioned before, whatever is in the hedgehog's bedding can easily travel up his nose and into the respiratory tract owing to his ground-hugging profile. This way, sawdust and other similar organic substances that have the tendency to decompose of crumble quickly have to be avoided. Not to mention, some of these may contain pathogenic substances your hedgie may acquire.

Gravel.

For obvious reasons, a bedding should be as soft as possible. Gravel is only suited for terrariums involving reptiles or tortoises.

Pine Shavings.

This may be most commonly used bedding material for pets. They can be easily obtained, absorb urine adequately, and manufactured/sold by most pet companies.

However, aside from having the same Plicatic Acid as cedar, they also contain Abietic Acid which are present when not properly treated (heat cured), causing similar problems as cedar shavings do in the long run. While there are some companies that meticulously treat their pine shavings in a way that is best for smaller pets, may still purchase bulk packages that are originally sold for use with livestock, obviously of inferior quality. Pine shavings can also easily accumulate dust that may cause respiratory issues.

If ever you will be using these (i.e., when you have no choice left), make sure at least that the pine shavings have been kiln dried. This can only be used safely as bedding of the hedgie's cage has good ventilation. There are also some types of pine shaving bedding that contain lower levels of most aromatic hydrocarbons.

Other Wood Products

Of course, Pine and Cedar are far from being the only choices. There are several wood shavings that can be used as hedgehog bedding. The more common ones are enumerated below.

Aspen.

Aspen shavings have been deemed relatively safe to use as hedgie bedding. It is also inexpensive and can be easily found at most retailers. It is considered by many as a better substitute for other types of wood shavings, and have been said to be a better material for hedgehogs suffering from skin sensitivities (although, of course, some hedgehogs may still be allergic to it).

On the downside, Aspen cannot be as effective in controlling odor, unlike most other bedding materials. The texture can be quite rough and coarse, and hedgehogs may not find it as comfortable - in fact, there are some products where the roughness is very near to those of splinters that these may injure the hedgie when it is curled into its ball. Larger, flakier shavings may be more ideal, but it can be very hard to find.

Pellet Wood.

There are a lot of pelleted wood options for hedgehog bedding purposes, made of different types of wood. This form offers many advantages. In fact, even pelleted pine (despite all its long-term effects) has been said to be superior in terms of accessibility, effectiveness, and cost when compared to other products.

There are also those products that are not purely made from pine. They may be made from some blend of other soft woods that can sometimes be irritating to the hedgie.

Aspen pellets also exist, and may be a better alternative for those who do not want to risk the pine variety.

One thing to remember is to use a larger dish or crock whenever dealing with pelleted wood as your bedding. This ensures that the pellets will not mix with the food itself.

One of the most outstanding properties of pelleted wood is that this material can draw the moisture from hedgehog droppings, eliminating a good part of the smell. When it gets wet, it decomposes into some sawdust-type composition that settles into the bottom of the cage. This makes it safer than other bedding products that decompose and do not settle appropriately. Settling allows the remaining pellets to remain on top.

Another upside is that the type of bedding will not stick to your pet's fur, in the way wooden shavings do.

On the downside, eating too much of this type of bedding can cause more digestive issues than the other ones. Also, maintenance is still needed since things might get dusty once many of these pellets start breaking down.

Paper-based Products

For the environmentally conscious, there are also several products in the hedgehog bedding market that are made out of recycled paper.

Pelleted Newspaper. These are mostly made out of recycled newspapers. They are not odorous, and may appear to be the same size and similar shape as rabbit pellets.

One disadvantage of this type of product is that it has the tendency to expand when ingested. Also, since the item is the same dark gray as the newspaper from which it has been derived, it may make hedgie's bedding look unkempt. It may also serve as a camouflage that hides the color of any abnormal hedgehog droppings.

Fluffy Paper.

There are also manufacturers who opt to make products derived from wood pulp, making a lighter and fluffier version of the regular hedgehog bedding. These items are reportedly absorbent, and do not disintegrate when they get wet, unlike wooden pellets. It has been seen to be dust-free, but these are also isolated reports that the item can accumulate a lot of dust. This might vary depending on the quality of the individual product. It could also be affected by the burrowing habits of the hedgie itself. There may be several colors to choose from.

On the downside, it has not been found to be as effective in controlling the odor produced by the hedgie's droppings. For best control of odor, it is recommended that the cage be cleaned around twice in a day or as necessary. Though there is relatively little chance that this product will be ingested along with the hedgehog's food, it is also advised that the owner keep a close watch – being made of paper, this product expands when wet. It could also easily cause intestinal damage. Another downside is on the maintenance part. Since the product is lightweight, it may easily be knocked out of the wire cage when the hedgie goes around his day to day activities. Since it clings, it may be difficult to pick up with a vacuum cleaner.

Newsprint. Plain newsprint of the unprinted variety could be used as sheets to be a liner at the bottom of the hedgehog's cage. Many newspapers will actually freely give or sell for a cheap price the print paper towards the end of the newsprint rolls.

However, though this product may win in terms of cost, it may not provide a good bedding for your hedgehog since it lacks a majority of the advantages offered by traditional products.

Fabrics

For hedgehogs with issues of sensitivity when being moved from one bedding to another, it may best suit them to provide a fabric bedding. This type is most commonly recommended for those whose pets show allergies from different products. It is recyclable, aside from being easily be stored. Also, it is less likely this will harbor mites and other pets. No splinters, small pieces, or dust will fall out of the wire cage.

However, as always, care must also be undertaken when dealing with these products. Loose threads may appear at the edges that can pose danger to your pet by wrapping around their feet or toes. It has been found that a small stretch of thread is enough to cause damage in the extremity affected, over a period of 6 hours. Many a hedgehog foot has been amputated because of this simple reason. As such, all fabric items inside the hedgie's home should be checked for any loose threads. They may not be there when you first put them in, but they may appear over time.

This may also not be the best option for those hedgies that have not been sufficiently litter-trained. The absorbency of the material can easily be changed by the fabric softeners, coupled with the newness of the item when first being used. Newer fabrics, especially when treated with fabric softeners, would normally cause urine to build up in puddles. Accessories may also be tripped by a playful hedgehog, as such are easily slid on a cloth lining.

Some owners opt to protect their pets from any "fragrance irritations" by washing the fabrics with detergents especially suited to sensitive skin. Extra pieces of the material can also be provided, so that your hedgehog doesn't burrow into the lining itself. Accessories could also use a Velcro lining to avoid slipping. Light colors are most advisable for an easy way to easily see changes in the urine or stool. The use of bleach when washing should also be avoided as much as possible, since the product has been known to degrade the fabric material.

Vellux.

Some hedgehog owners utilize Vellux blankets as bedding for their hedgehog cages. This may be separated into pieces, allowing it to fit in of the cage itself. They can be interchanged and washed every two days, and then reused. They have the added advantage of standing up to many washing repetitions, without unraveling even in the hands of curious scratching hedgies. But like other fabrics, bleach can break it down so other alternatives must be looked into.

Fleece.

This type of material can easily be found and is relatively inexpensive. There are anti-pill fleece that could last longer than the traditional fleece. Make sure to follow the washing instructions of the manufacturer in order to avoid the breaking down of this material.

Crib Liners.

You may also use the thick pads that are available in baby sections of a majority of department stores. If you used to have them and would not need them anymore, this is a practical option.

Other Materials

The beauty of hedgehog beddings is the extremely wide variety of materials one can use. In the end, these can actually rely on the owner's imagination.

Corncob Bedding.

These is a relatively inexpensive material, although be careful to make sure that the cage is clean at all times. It may retain different fluids including urine because of its organic properties. It can also be eaten quickly by molds. Keep in mind that molds can cause respiratory ailments. Frequent maintenance can help decrease the instances of mold formation.

Corncob can also stick to a hedgehog's genitalia – it can be caught up in a hedgie's penile sheath. From this, it can be dragged inside. This can cause irritation and raw sores, culminating in a problem in your pet's urination.

Pellet Straw or Wheat Grass.

These products usually are carried by a variety of manufacturers. It is usually said to be dust-free, and can be good at absorption. It is usually heat-treated, aiding in the elimination of mites and many other pests.

They are greatly biodegradable. They can even be flushed down the drain or toilet. Based on these qualities, many veterinarians actually recommend this over pelleted wood based on these qualities.

Indoor-Outdoor Carpets.

Indoor-outdoor carpets are good to use as cage liners. Materials such as Astroturf can easily be cleaned, and yet must be regularly observed for traveling edges. These beddings are best for pets which are trained in a litter box.

Disposable Liners.

Pads that were made to be utilized for housebreaking dogs are best used to combat germs and other pathogens, and are best for injured or sick hedgies.

Cleaning The Cage

A hedgie's cage can be made of different materials. It can be the common wire cage, or a six-inch deep pan. It may have wire sidings, or may be made of plastic. Glass aquariums and wading pools may also be used. One of the most common requirements is that the cage should at least be four square feet in area, and must contain an eating area, a litter box, a sleeping box, and an exercise wheel. They are generally placed in an area protected from draft or direct sunlight.

As mentioned before, hedgehogs have a very keen sense of smell. If something smells bad to you, it will smell much worse to your pet. It is best not to use any deodorizers of perfumes when cleaning the hedgie cages, as they may cause adverse reactions. It is very important to completely clean not only the beddings but the bottom of the cage itself. This is applicable especially for plastic bottoms, as plastic can absorb odors. For those opting to use a safer, more natural way of cleaning the cage, it is recommended to use a two-step cleaning process that involves using hydrogen peroxide and white vinegar. This process has been found by many to effectively remove not only more odors but also more bacteria than bleach. Make sure not to pre-mix the two substances. One product can be sprayed on, and the other one wiped on with a rag while the first layer is still wet.

Chapter 9 - Conclusion

I hope you enjoyed reading my book on how to keep hedgehogs as amazing pets! We hope you learned a lot of valuable things.

Finally, if you enjoyed this book, please take the time to share your thoughts and **post a review on Amazon**. It'd be greatly appreciated!

Thank you!

Check Out My Other Books

Go ahead and check out the other great books I've published!

<u>Amazing Facts and Myths About Camel Spiders</u>

<u>The Amazing African Clawed Frog as a Pet</u>

Please feel free to contact me with your comments, good or bad!

<u>greenslopesdirect@gmail.com</u>

Many Thanks,

Hathai.

Index

Index

How to Keep an Amazing Hedgehog Pet

Lightning Source UK Ltd.
Milton Keynes UK
UKHW02f0808191117
312965UK00009B/500/P